From
Fear to
Speak

ALEXIA FRANKLIN

Paperback: 978-1-965632-25-3
Hardcover: 978-1-965632-47-5
eBook: 978-1-965632-26-0
Library of Congress Control Number: 2024919988

Ordering Information:

Prime Seven Media
518 Landmann St.
Tomah City, WI 54660

Printed in the United States of America

Table of Contents

Acknowledgments

I would like to thank the following people

Shirley Swinchatt

Shirley Thompson

Dorothy Kenward

A very special thank you to Amy & Frizz who
was a very frightened dog when we met but
now it's are we going out? No? Come on!

Pauline White

Tony Robbins

Wayne Dyer

Joe Vitale

Hay House

My bank who sent someone to help with the fraud.

Introduction

Six years ago, I had all I wanted. I had moved house the year before from the country to the town, as it was easier for me to get around. I just could not settle into my new home and now my health was deteriorating. I was always tired and didn't want to go out.

I was always busy doing something, even when I was not working. I had given up my cleaning business. I was going to the gym at least three times a week and I had lots of friends who I liked to meet with, but I was just too tired even to want to talk with them on the phone. I started to shut myself away indoors.

I visited my GP surgery, who just dismissed me, saying it was probably a virus. But I wasn't getting better. I could only walk for a few minutes and then I had to sit down.

Earlier that year, I had met a lady with a white dog with some black markings. He was continually barking and he seemed to be frightened of everything. The lady and I chatted for a few minutes and then she told me she had gotten him from a local rescue centre. We went our separate ways, but I thought about that dog all day.

Many months passed and I had been back to the doctors many times, as my health was deteriorating. I was still getting told there was nothing wrong. So, I thought I needed to do something about this. Maybe I could connect with someone on the Internet, as that would not be as tiring as talking. I would only chat when I felt like it. Perhaps I could help others, and just maybe it could help me change how I was feeling.

I got to talking with someone I thought was in the US Army. By now, I felt so depressed that I was not capable of making sensible decisions. He was a scammer, but at the time I could not see this. It just seemed reasonable to meet someone who might need more help than me.

Over six months, he scammed me of all my money. My health was getting worse and I ended up in hospital just before Christmas. When I eventually got back home, I felt I must try to get out of this. It might help me feel better.

So, the next morning I made up my mind I would do a few minutes' walk in the park opposite my house. As I opened my front door and stepped outside, right in front of me was the white and black dog that I had met all those months ago. He was barking, but this time he was heading straight for a bus that was coming down the road towards them. I grabbed the lady's coat and the dog's lead. I told the dog to behave and the owner thanked me.

She said, "Don't touch him. He may bite."

We got to talking and she told me that her name was Amy and the dog was Frizz. She told me she was trying to cross the road over to the park and I asked if I could join her, as I was going to try a short walk there. She said it would be nice to have someone to walk with.

We talked about Frizz and how frightened he was of just about everything. This was his fourth home. He was not happy in the park, so I said, "Bring him to my house, as I have a safe garden where he can run around."

So that's what we did. After Amy and I had talked for a bit, Frizz was asking to come in. She said yes, he could come in—but if he was a problem, she would take him home.

Looking back now, this was a turning point. Frizz and Amy would see me most days. We would go to the park and then come back to my house, where Frizz would run from the house to the garden. Still, my health was not getting any better. The scam now meant I would lose my home, and I would be living on the streets.

The doctor had finally found out what was wrong with me, but to get the treatment, I needed to have an address. Amy insisted I move in with her and Frizz for a while. After some persuading, I agreed to stay with them, On the day I moved in with what few things I could take with me, I told myself that I would change how I felt—my thoughts.

It was not easy for me to write this book for two reasons. The first is that I'm dyslexic. The second is that it meant confronting my past and letting go of what happened to me.

I have rebuilt my life and cleared all my debt from the fraud, and I am now in the process of finding a home. I would like to share with you how I did this. It will take some work from you to do the same, but it is all simple.

From Fear to Peace

I wrote this book because I wanted something easy to read

That was simple to understand.

How I could change my life from fear to love?

Friends told me I needed to put into a book what I did and why.

It has taken me a long time to put it down on paper,

As I had to write about what happened to me. It was not easy to do,

but it has made me see things clearly.

Please don't ever give up on life and your dreams.

It's Free to Change

My first tip is that it's free to change. Are you ready to make a change? This is the question I asked myself. You are reading this book, so you are looking for ways to make life better.

My second tip is that it's up to you to make the change. This book can't do it for you. It is an account of what I did. I know these things work because I have done them. I assume you have read the introduction and know my story, so let's get to how I did it, right now.

The change was simple enough, but like everything, it takes a commitment. I had to make a promise to myself that I would keep going and that I would change things no matter what it took. Everything that I did was straightforward and simple to do. I had to look at myself and be honest with myself. I had to ask what I was feeling. I was tense, and my breathing was laboured. I was frightened. I asked myself if I wanted this pain to end.

I answered yes: I did want the pain to stop. Then I asked myself what would happen if I changed my breathing. Slowly I changed the way I was breathing by sitting quietly and watching it. Slowly I began to calm down and that made me feel better. So I took another look at how I was feeling and asked myself, did things feel as bad as before?

My answer was no. I felt calmer and my mind was clearer. So, I asked myself how I could stay that way. I needed it to be simple and easy to do. Well, I thought, I have to breathe. It's free. It's simple to change my breath. I felt better when I took control of my breathing.

Five simple words that I kept in my mind were *change what you think about.* When you do this, what you think about will change. I will come back to this thought throughout the book.

Taking Charge

The day after Amy took me in, when I was struggling to make my way upstairs to bed, I said, "Okay, this has to stop."

Amy asked, "What do you mean?"

I replied, "I have to change what I'm thinking—how I feel about the fraud. The tears and fear have to go. I have to take responsibility for my life. I have to change my thoughts. I have to let go of all the feelings coming up from inside me."

Afterward, I said to myself, You need to be honest and take a good look at yourself. How does what you are thinking make you feel? What emotions are you feeling?

I started to write down everything that came into my thoughts. When I looked at what I'd written, it was very negative. Could I find some positive words instead?

crying

alone

anger

hurt

loss

calm

alive

action

healed

loving

Taking each of the positive words, I reflected on how it made me feel.

- *Calm: I could think clearly.*

- *Alive: Breathing came to my mind, so I could use the breath to be calm.*

- *Action: I would get fit. Walking is free—I can do that.*

- *Healing: Did I need to hold on to the past? No, I could let it go.*

- *Loving: I could love myself?*

That last one would take a bit of thinking as to how I could love myself.

Everything I was doing was free. I didn't need money to do any of it, just time, believing in myself and commitment to making a change in myself. Loving myself was the hardest to do because of the pain I was feeling. But once I had the words in my head, I found that love changes everything.

Change how you think and what you think about will change. I needed to be aware of the words I was using and how I was using them, as this changed not only how I felt but also how other people would interact with me.

It's Simple

This is exactly how I did it.

1. *I changed negative thoughts to positive.* Here's an easy way to get started: compliment a stranger. This must come from the heart. "Excuse me, but I love your top." It will make the other person feel good.

2. *I looked at how I felt inside.* After giving that compliment, I now feel good inside, as I have brightened someone's day.

3. *I moved from fear to peace.* I would do something I had not wanted to do. For me, that was talking to people about the fraud. This took away the fear. I did this, and I began to feel some peace.

4. *Next, I moved to harmony.* I felt better, as I was doing more and putting my life back together. This gave me both harmony and peace of mind. I was changing to a positive way of thinking, which meant I could take control of my life. Watching what I thought about was vital to the change, as it was my connection to greater things. I watched what words I used in my speech, thinking and writing. I determined to use positive thoughts and positive words.

5. *Finally, I came to love.* Now I could begin to love myself. This did bring changes to my life. It brings me back to the song "Love Changes Everything." Can I take this on? I will go out and enjoy life. Every morning, I ask, "How can I serve you?" The name you use is up to you; four possibilities are God, Buddha, Ra and the Universe.

Looking Deeper

I needed to look deeper into how to change. So, I asked myself, *What is it in me that I need to change?* I needed to let go of my past, as that time was gone. I needed to deal with now. This was what I could change right now, right this minute.

I used many different techniques to help me empower my mind and take control of my thoughts. These are some of the first things I did:

- I relaxed, even if only for five minutes.
- I supported others, which reminded me we all have things we find hard to deal with.
- I meditated, something which can be done while walking to work.
- I said, "I am happy. I am going to have a great day."
- I said to myself, "I love you—I will love you always."
- I told myself, "I am going to have a great day. I see a perfect day."

Question: Is he happy or sad?

The Shift

Wondering how to change your mind? Let's look at some examples:

1. "I'll go shopping? Mmm, maybe not. No, I'll go tomorrow."
   What is wrong with this? Indecision and hesitation. Let's try again.

2. "I am going shopping today. I am going to enjoy it."
   This is decisive. You must be clear about what you want. It's essential. You must stay focused, keep a check on your thoughts, and clear negative thoughts.

3. "I want to have positive thoughts."
   Can I ask you a question? What thoughts would you want to have? As you are reading this book, you must be looking to change. Okay, let's go for it.

4. "Oh yes, I can change how I think."
   I would like to ask you: Can you change how you feel?

5. "Yes, I can. I can change how I feel."
   Change how you think and your life will change. Change how you feel and your life will change. I said it was simple. Yes, it's up to you. Do the work and that's it.

From Negative to Positive

*B*e careful what you think about, what you say and how you say it. This is important. It is very powerful. It can change how you feel but you have to work at it. Here are some words that we use without thinking that can change from negative to positive.

Negative words

angry

broken

can't

damaged

enraged

fear

hate

impossible

jealous

lousy

Positive words

action

brave

courageous

delight

existing

free

happy

instant

joy

lovely

These ten negative words we use every day can be changed to positive by changing how we think and changing what we say and how we say it. Take control of your thoughts to go from sad to good to great.

Ho'oponopono

I will say here that all the things that helped me came from the Internet or books. I wrote this so I could quickly find what I needed. The first and most important thing was to love myself. It was also the simplest thing I used to let go of my past.

I first read about Ho'oponopono in Joe Vitale's book *At Zero*. How did it help? It taught me three things:

1. How to love myself
2. How to let go of my past
3. How to make a move away from pain and hate

I had to let go of my past and change the hate to love, peace and harmony.

Ho'oponopono is simple to do and easy to remember. You can do it anywhere. Remember these four easy phrases to say in your head:

1. I'm sorry.
2. I love you.
3. Please forgive me.
4. Thank you.

Whatever came up that was a negative thought, I would change it. Then I would look at what I was feeling and say to myself:

1. I'm sorry.
2. I love you.
3. Please forgive me.
4. Thank you.

I would keep saying these words until I felt at peace. Yes, I am still saying them now.

What these words mean to me when I'm saying them:

I'm sorry is asking forgiveness

Please forgive me for any wrongs I have done

I love you thank you to God, Buddha, Divine

There is much more I could say about Ho'oponopono. I am not an expert in it, but it works for me. If you want to know more, read Joe Vitale's book or look up Dr Ihaleakala Hew Len, PhD. The important thing here is that you must keep working on *you*. This is how I made the change in myself. Yes, it is constant and ongoing. I work at it all the time.

Giving

Giving is an essential part of making your move to feeling good inside and out. What do I mean by giving? It's making time for you. We are always being asked to help and yes, it is good to help others. It is a great thing to do but it's vital that you do not forget to take care of yourself. You're not giving your best.

If you're wondering how to give, here is a simple way to get started. Take five minutes in the morning before you start your day and say, "I am going to have a great day." See your day going the way you want it.

Yes, there may be things that come up that we don't expect. We can choose how we react to them. Taking time for yourself will give you a chance to clear all the busy clutter that comes up in your thoughts and feelings. Let them go before you start your day.

Here are three more ways to be happy.
I am happy, healthy, wealthy and well.
I will love you always.
Fear is only as big as you let it, so let it go.
Love is always with me.

Challenge

I set myself the challenge of rebuilding my life. This meant talking to myself and asking: "Do you want life to change?" Ask yourself these three questions:

1. Will I do whatever it takes?
2. Can I do whatever it takes to make this change?
3. What will I do right now to make the change?

These questions are essential to making the change. I would be letting myself down if I did not take on the challenge to be happy and love myself,

Did I make a move to love myself? To be happy, take life on, and have fun? Yes, I did. Can I ask you, are you ready to take the challenge? Remember, this is a question you have asked of yourself, so you are letting yourself down if you break the commitment.

Will you commit to the challenge?

Five Easy Ways to Start the Day

1. Take three deep breaths in and out. You can do this while getting up or while having your first cup of coffee or tea or even on your way to work.

2. For a five-minute meditation use breathing to help clear your mind.

3. Take in a deep breath, let it go and say to yourself: "I love you, always. I am going to have a great day."

4. This is something I do every day: ask "How can I serve you?" to God, the universe, Buddha, or whatever name works for you. This takes away all the busy things going on in your mind, and then you can start to look for ways you can make your day go well. It also starts you thinking about how you can make other people's day go well.

5. Look in the mirror and say "I love you" out loud. It can be hard to do this, but it does make you feel good in mind and body. The first place you can do this is while getting washed. You're usually in front of the mirror and that is an excellent time to say "I love you." It can take a bit of practice to stand in front of the mirror. Do this and stick with it.

Looking Deeper

*L*et's look at other things I used to help me move on. One was music. I used this in three ways: to relax, to sleep, and to calm myself. For meditation, I might use a combination of quiet or nature sounds, like birdsong or water.

I also use music to wake myself up, give myself more energy and make myself feel good. I like something I can sing along with. One of my favourites is The 1812 Overture as it has everything that works for me to clear my mind, emotions and feelings, but what do you think it does not have?

Find what works for you. It's all out there, but it's up to you to take it on. Will you take life on?

One simple thing I do if I'm meeting people is to take time to think about what I will wear. This is important, as it makes me feel good and that helps people feel comfortable around me. Colour is essential for formal meetings or interviews. Dark colours like black, grey, and navy can be oppressive and make you feel sad. Bright colours can give you energy. Pastel or lighter colours are calming or relaxing.

Colour affects how people react to you, so it is worth taking time to think about what colours make you feel good. See the colour chart on the next page for more information.

Two Things That Helped Me

We think all the time. Even when we are asleep, our subconscious is working, so training the mind helps mentally, physically and emotionally. Here are two more things I use to control my thoughts. They are not free, but they work for me.

Holosync Therapy

Put simply, Holosync therapy is music with a difference. You need headphones for it to work. Without headphones, it's just sound. With headphones, the sound is slightly different in each ear.

I found that some sounds in music upset me. One was birdsong; another was the sound of water. Using Holosync, I found that these irritations were gone and they have not come back. I also found it helped with my balance. I used it when meditating and I am still using it. You can get a free download to try. I found it just by chance on the Internet.

Return to Love Frequencies

Return to Love Frequencies look like crystals but are made with sound in them. I found them very powerful in helping me to let go of my past. I have also used the Frequencies to help other people with fascinating reactions. I have put them in this book because they are easy to use. I am still using them now. I came across these at a meeting and was sent a book all about them as a gift then I did some research on them. I spent two days in a workshop about them.

Health and Well-Being

Look at what you are thinking and feeling. What do you need to change to achieve good health and well- being? What is well-being and why is it important? Well-being is paramount to how we feel inside, how we see life and how much energy we have. It can affect everything we do, including our work, how we view life and how others react to us.

Can you use well-being to change how you feel? How would you change to feel well? If you are out of balance mentally or physically your well-being is not balanced. There are many things that can affect you. Here are the most common things I have felt: fear, loss, hurt, stress, anxiety and depression. These feelings come up in everyone at some point.

How did I achieve well-being? By taking control of my thoughts, feelings and emotions. Here's a tip: take small steps. Pick one thing in your mind that is making you worry or feel wrong and change it, now.

One thing you can do is say: "I am going to have a great day at work." I take a few minutes to see my day as I want it to go. Yes, some things come up that I didn't expect but because my head, heart and feelings are balanced I feel good. My well-being is excellent. I can deal with what comes up.

As an example of how things can change if you are happy with life, there was a misunderstanding with a customer who was very upset and shouting at me. I listened and then said, quietly, "Please do not shout at me." Then I listened to what the person had to say. By the time that individual left, everyone was happy. The customer spent more money and would not take the change, so I gave it to charity.

Another thing I do for my health and well-being is take care about what I eat and drink. I plan my meals so they are simple to make. Most of my meals are cooked in only two pans, are planned by what they cost, can be used for a second meal the next day and can be cooked in the oven or microwave. I like to drink I do have a particular tea and coffee because I find it works for me. It is called Organo and I do have to order it as you can't just go buy it in the shops. You are welcome to contact me, I can send you some to try.

When my life was turned upside down I made a promise that I would still find time to help others. I became a volunteer for a charity and gave my time. Now I give financially as well. I have cleared all my debts from the fraud. I have rebuilt my life and now I am looking for the right home. So, I know it can be done. Focus on love, peace and patience. I now have bought my new home in Cambridgeshire.

From Fear to Peace

There are two reasons I chose the title. The first is because fear is what I felt after the fraud. All my money and my home were gone. Where was I going to live? How was I going to clear the debt?

The second reason I called the book *From Fear to Peace* is because when I was writing it, I had a feeling of fear as this was the biggest challenge I could take on and as I am dyslexic. But there is a peace here and a love of writing I now have. I kept this book short, as when I was ill, I could not focus on anything for more than a few minutes. When I talked to people who were not well they all said the same thing; that they could only do things for a few minutes.

The important thing here is that I contacted the police about the fraud. I talked to my bank, and my creditors worked out a plan to clear my debt. People who can help include Victim Support Samaritans. They cannot help with money, but talking is the starting point to peace, love, and well-being.

This is where the fun begins because I changed my thoughts. Things changed, some small, but it was fun. I was going to London and I saw myself having a good time. I just got on the train. When I had to change trains as I got onto the platform the train came.

The following poem was written by taking words from

Faith Fear to Free

Faith is with you always,

So why do you change it to fear

When freedom is always inside you?

You know you have nothing to fear.

Faith is always with you.

You know you can always change it

To be free.

Freedom is always inside you,

So you know you have nothing to fear.

Faith is always with you;

You know you have nothing to fear.

the missing link to change

I talked of the importance of the words and what we think about and how we react to what has happened to us and what is around us, there is an important element that I left out in the original book what is it the planet or better known as mother Earth why is this important because this is where all life begins and ends,

How do you use the earth to help you, every thing we do is connected like a chain liked fence lets show you what i mean

Earth air fire water when any one of these is out of balance

you can have flooding drought and fires can burn out of control, why does this matter because every resource we use have come from this planet including the water we drink the food we eat the clothes we wear so being kind to the planet is being kind to you.

This one step of respecting the planet will come back to you

how can you be kind to the earth keep it clean only take what you need reuse repair recycle it has bought me more joy and help to people who can not buy new we are not over using the earth resources you will be helping to control global warming.

This could take book on its own but i wrote this book to be a quick start to change that is different for everyone

Testimonials

I have never known anyone as brave as my dear friend Alexia. To coin a phrase, she has been though the mill and back. Her life suddenly turned upside down and she lost everything she ever treasured and owned, including her home which had a detrimental effect on her health, both physically and mentally.

At times, it seemed there was no point of return and I feared for her life. Then she turned a corner. Through spiritual practice and inner strength I watched as she waged war against the people who had done this to her. She wasn't going to let them beat her. It was no mean feat and she still works on herself today

It is only right and fitting that Alexia has written this amazing self-help book, *From Fear to Peace* not only as part of her therapy progress but as one of the most straightforward and easy reference self-help tools I have come across. This is an everyday book for everyday life situations.

- Shirley Swinchatt

When I first got know Lexie, she was looking forward to getting married and emigrating to Canada. She was obviously poorly and could barely manage to walk around the park. I recognised a fellow thyroid suffer and suggested she query this with her doctor. This had a good result, and she began to pick up.

She would come to my house and help with my dog training a couple of days a week. The dog always sent her packing at 7 p.m., pushing her off the sofa and guiding her to the door. We decided that he had brains and started setting him tasks, mostly fetching things for us.

Shortly before she was due to move, the money went into the bank five minutes later. She had been scammed. She hit rock bottom. We moved all her belongings into two garages, and she slept in my spare room.

It has taken a long time and a lot of positive thinking, but she has found a part-time job and has enough money saved to buy a house and move on. What a journey!

As for the dog, he is currently scanning the television adverts looking at sofas. Why would a dog find sofas interesting? Unless he is a lot more clever than we give him credit for.

- Amy

About the Author

*A*lexia Franklin is from Newham East Sussex, she went straight from school to work as a nurse, married John, started a cleaning business then John got cancer for the fourth time and died so she went back to school to study health and well-being then became ill, was defrauded, lost all her money, home and nearly her life.